What To Do At 62

Stop Leaving Hundreds of Thousands of Dollars of Social Security Benefits on the Table

Learn Why Over 80% of all Age Eligible Social Security Pensioners are Missing Out on an Average of over $212,000 of Income Benefits!

From Best Selling Author
Chuck Oliver

Here's What's Inside...

5   Introduction

7   **What to Do at 62!**

7   **Why Is 62 a Significant Age?**

10 **Why Is There so Much Confusion About What to Do at 62?**

15 **Here Are the Four Greatest Threats to People's Retirement...**

21 **Here Are Some of the Mistakes People Make When They Approach 62...**

23 **Here Are the Five Biggest Traps to Retirement...**

33 **Why It's not Too Late for You...**

37 **What Is One Filing Strategy Most Couples Do not Know that Could Cost Them Over $200K?**

41 **Here's Exactly How the Social Security Pay Maximization Plan Works...**

43 **Here's Exactly How to Get Your Social Security Pay Maximization Plan...**

Dedication:

Being blessed in serving consumers with direction to discover and uncover their Hidden Wealth.
I dedicate to my amazing wife and wonderful sons.

Introduction

April 2014
Orlando, Florida

For almost two decades, I have been
concerned and frustrated at having
to use social security in my clients' retirement
income planning. The uncertainty of whether or not
social security would even be around when my
clients retired and needed or desired always left
myself and clients uneasy.

I must confess, I attacked social security and learned I
was wrong. I know now benefits will be paid and
there are proven strategies in how to maximize
pension payout benefits. The reality is that the top
25% of retirees count on 30% of their total income to
come from social security pension payments.

I vowed to find the best strategies for maximum
income solutions, so I went in search of an answer.
Imagine my surprise to find the answer directly from
a Social Security benefits expert.

I have worked to become one of the few retirement
income specialists to become an expert on social
security benefit filing strategies. I started educating
clients on how to retire with the most retirement
income possible by helping clients discover and
uncover all areas of their Hidden Wealth.

As a result, I've been able to share this knowledge with clients enabling them to increase their benefit payouts over double what they were expecting, and for some of my clients, we have even quadrupled their results.

One of the rarely understood strategies I found allows my clients to avoid being taxed on their Social Security Benefits.

Another strategy designs a tax-free income that continues for the surviving spouse. The lower of the two social security benefits is lost after the first spouse passes away and consumers do not account for this loss.

And lastly, how to avoid being taxed up to 85% on social security benefits.

Enjoy the book education!

I hope it educates you and helps change the way you think about and strategically plan your Social Security Benefit and encourages you to take the unique steps to maximize your pension income payouts.

Here is To You Discovering and Uncovering Your Hidden Wealth,

Chuck Oliver

Best-Selling Author & National Radio Host

What to Do at 62!

Susan: Hi, this is Susan Austin and with me is Chuck Oliver best-selling author and national radio host from sunny Orlando, Florida. Welcome Chuck.

Chuck: Thank you very much, Susan. It's great to be speaking with you.

Why Is 62 a Significant Age?

Susan: Today we're talking about <u>What to Do at 62</u>. Why is 62 such a significant age for people Chuck?

Chuck: Susan it comes down to understanding there are over 80 different filing strategies that can be used when filing for Social Security. Approximately 10,000 people a day turn 62 and will continue to do so each year for the next 19 years. This has put huge strain on social security as people need this income source to maintain their standard of living or want to make sure they can collect some or all of which they paid into the government over their work careers. There is a lot of market data research revealing; at least one spouse will live at least three decades beyond 62. So people are being forced to start looking at their Social Security benefits and they really don't know whether they should take their benefits at 62 or should they wait. I think a big concern is the fear of maintaining their lifestyle. Having the purchasing power to do what they want to do when they want to do and really enjoy their retirement. The biggest fear is the fear of running out of money before running out of life with many wanting to make sure they have the income source of social security locked in to help support their income needs in retirement. We find many people just want to make sure they trigger their benefit before the government changes the rules and pushes back the qualifying age or reduces the formula for how the benefits are paid out.

People don't know what the best pension benefit payout strategies are or the loss impact if they elect to take those benefits now versus waiting, but it's not always an easy question to answer. I think too when they hit their early 60's, it's sort of a wake-up call, and they start to look at this and say, "I better get really serious about what I'm doing to plan for my retirement income."

We find a large number of baby boomers have not saved a tremendous amount of money towards their retirement for various reasons. One reason is because baby boomers are considered the sandwich generation meaning they are taking care of parents and children and are being squeezed between these two responsibilities which leave little extra time or money to plan or save. There are many that have done a good job in savings. However we find these strong boomer and retiree savers have most of all their retirement money they have saved trapped in IRA's from old work 401k's and many are concerned over the taxes they will have to pay when they elect to distribute money from these accounts. What we find many forget is the tax they will owe is not just on the amount they distribute from their IRA's that the government counts as taxable income but also the fact that the government also taxes them up to 85% on their social security benefits as a result of the withdrawals people make from their IRA accounts to supplement their retirement income. This is a result of really double taxation because we already pay social security tax on our earned wages and then to have to be taxed again on our income we deferred causes many clients great concern of running out of money due to higher taxes in retirement that many paid while working.

I think they feel confused about what to do and wonder, "What's the best path for me?" The reality is with people living so much longer and all of the uncertainty in the economy; I think this gets a lot of people motivated to focus on retirement planning at this age.

Susan: Age 62 is the earliest someone can claim Social Security benefits, is that right?

Chuck: Susan, 80% of eligible benefit recipients file for their benefits before their full retirement age (full Retirement Age referred to as FRA is age 66 for most) and most are not aware of other filing strategy options available to them that could cost them losing over $200,000 on average in lost payout benefits they could have collected. Yes, currently age 62 is the earliest one can file for benefits unless someone is widowed. If they're widowed, they actually could file for benefits as early as age 60.

Why Is There so Much Confusion About What to Do at 62?

Susan: Why is there so much confusion about whether or not they should start filing for Social Security at 62?

Chuck: One of the biggest concerns people have is the potential insolvency of Social Security. It seems to be people's biggest concern - will Social Security really be there for me? If I don't elect to start taking benefits now, could they push the earliest qualifying age further out? People are afraid if they don't take their Social Security benefits when they turn 62 they may be prevented from doing so when they need the money. This causes them stress.

The government is looking at pushing back qualifying ages. If your birth date is 1960 or after, to get full retirement benefits, has been pushed back from 66 and 2 months all the way out to full retirement age of 67 depending on their birth month. It can confuse people because the stated numbers are adjusted for cost of living with an annual 8% increase plus the cost of living. This is depending on how many years before the stated ages being reviewed are factored when someone officially reaches the filing years.

Here's one strategy many people need to really learn about before they lose the opportunity.

The president's fiscal-year 2015 budget includes language to "eliminate what some are calling aggressive Social Security-claiming strategies. This strategy allows people to strategize the timing of collection of Social Security benefits in order to maximize delayed retirement credits."

Under Social Security, married individuals are entitled to a retired worker benefit based on their own earnings and/or to a spousal benefit equal to one half of their spouse's benefit claimed at the full retirement age (currently 66). Until 2000, the Social Security Administration assumed that an individual claiming benefits was applying for all benefits to which he or she was entitled, compared the worker and spousal benefits, and automatically awarded the highest.

The Senior Citizen's Freedom to Work Act of 2000 changed the procedure. Under the new law, upon reaching the full retirement age, individuals can choose which benefit to receive. As a result, married individuals can claim a spousal benefit at 66 and switch to their own retired worker benefit at a later date. This approach allows a worker to begin claiming one type of benefit while still building up delayed retirement credits, which will result in a higher worker benefit later.

Remember when the majority of the thinking around Social Security was the reminder when we used to get that benefit statement around our birthday which would give a projection of what your benefits will be when you retire? Now, you have to actually go to the Social Security website (www.ssa.gov) to physically log on and download this form and now there are strategies that enable the average family benefit payout to increase over $200,000 by knowing what to do and when to do it!

This is a very simple process to create your own online account log in information and then it is easy for people to see their projected benefits and other information on the site. This is a good first step to become aware of what your projected benefits will be based on which age someone is looking to start their benefits.

The statement tells you your benefit at age 62; this is your projected pay out. If you take it at 66 or 67, it's this much. Then if you deferred all the way to 70, here's so much more you'd be able to collect. I think people are confused at when to start collecting their benefits since many are not sure what the best move is for themselves.

Many people ask me, "When I turn 62, do you think it's a good thing for me to elect to start to take Social Security benefits?" and our answer is always, "Well, it depends."

The Social Security Administration provides little help with this question. The department is there to take and process the requested order. They're not going to give you any strategy or review the cost of living and building out a lifetime income plan for somebody in retirement. They're just going to say, "If you elect 62, this is what you get. If you elect 66 or 67, this is what you get. If you elect 70 then this is what you get." It doesn't make them bad people. It's just they're not going to provide any helpful direction for people to make an informed decision. I think a lot of people are starting to realize, "Wow, if I really want to understand this, maybe there's more to this Social Security thing than just picking one of three age choices. What's behind door number 1, 2, or 3? One very important question is: "How will my benefits election impact me and my surviving spouse long term as a result of what I choose?" Many need reminded that the lower of the two benefits stops at the passing of the first spouse. The death benefit from Social Security is only 255.00 dollars. Couples desire a solution for this guaranteed income gap coming in the future.

Susan: Right. That's really why there's so much confusion here because people have to make a choice whether they want to start receiving benefits or delay and receive higher amount later. Then you have to add in the reality that benefits are lost with basically no death benefit protection of the lower benefit to the surviving spouse.

Chuck: Susan, 34% of retirees today have their sole income source come from Social Security. Today 42% is the average of all retirees' income coming from Social Security. The top 25% of retirees ages 65-69 have on average 30% of their income coming from Social Security!

The average monthly benefit payout is $1,250.00. When you elect 62, ultimately what you're electing for is only getting 75% of what is called your FRA, (your full retirement age) benefits. By definition, your FRA, your full retirement age benefit, if it is post 1960 will be 66 and a certain number of months out to age 67 for now. If you elect to take your benefits at age 62, what you're saying is *I need the money*. Not everyone realizes when they pick age 62 they're going to take a 25% hit to what the benefit would've been had they waited till their full retirement age. Many times it will make sense for one spouse to elect benefits.

Electing the wrong time or not knowing some of the strategies that will enable you to really increase your social security payout becomes a big deal. If you elect to take it early, and you technically don't need it, you can be taxed up to 85% of that benefit.

We find a lot of people are not aware of this. They don't realize if they lost their job or if they need extra income because they're taking care of parents or children and they elect to take their benefits now, they're going to lose 25% of what they could receive at full retirement age. In addition, depending on how much their household income is, they could be taxed up to anywhere between 50% and as high as 85% on their social security benefit.

Bottom line, there is a lot of uncertainty and confusion with people out there on trying to figure out what are the consequences if I do this now versus if I do it later. I think it's really a shock to people how much less money they're going to get and how much higher they're going to be taxed as a result of not really knowing when it makes the most sense to file for benefits.

Here Are the Four Greatest Threats to People's Retirement...

Susan: Let's talk about this some more, so they have a better understanding of what they're up against.

Chuck: We have an acronym that we use called T.I.M.E. to help people understand what is at stake and to help give them some retirement peace of mind. T.I.M.E. stands for what I believe are the four greatest threats to people's retirement. 'T' stands for _taxation_. Currently the government can tax as much as 85% of your social security. Soon it could be 100%. People just don't realize how much they're ultimately losing to taxation on their Social security, their IRA's, prior 401k's, pensions, etc...

Taxes are a really big deal especially when someone realizes if your Social Security can be taxed up to 85%, ultimately you're only getting 80% of your benefit after taxes are factored. This is not made clear to an individual who is making their Social Security selections. There is nobody at the Social Security Administration saying _are you sure you want to do this? Have you considered the tax ramifications of your choice?_

The 'I' in T.I.M.E. stands for _Inflation_ which is a huge threat to people's retirement income and maintaining their preferred standard of lifestyle.

The government claims because there was so little inflation in 2010 and 2011 they fully suspended any cost of living adjustment to Social Security. People need to understand the government's inflation calculation excludes food and energy so the perception to the public is that inflation is so low there is no need to increase the benefit payout. The Government calculation is one approach in preserving the solvency of Social Security as they use as a way to manipulate the public into believing with so little inflation there is no need to increase their monthly benefit to keep pace with the cost of living.

Take a look at any family's liability side of their balance sheet and I'll promise the two largest items on the liability side of the family balance sheet is food and energy. The fact we can exclude those two items is really a manipulation of the math. It's a way for the government to indirectly say, "We can limit what we pay out because we're not going to give an increase for cost of living." For 2013, they came around and gave an increase which was a whopping 1.5%.

That 1.5% increase translates to a whopping $17.00 average increase to the monthly Social Security benefit. I can assure you gas, groceries, utilities et cetera has gone up more than $17 a month. Do you really want to leave it up to the government to gauge when they choose and how much they choose to raise the cost of living adjustments on Social Security especially when almost half of all retirees' income comes from the source of Social Security? There are key strategies to take control over our Social Security so we can have our own guaranteed income increases with a proven protected pension income guarantee.

Here's a graph which shows the Cost Of Living Adjustment (COLA) so you can see how the COLA keeps getting smaller and smaller.

```
COLA Comparison

(Not a Favorable Pattern Forming)

        Last 30 years   - 4.0%

        Last 20 years   - 2.4%

        Last 10 years   - 2.5%

        Last  5 years   - 1.36%
```

There are other strategies in being able to use social security benefits to build a tax free lifetime income plan and avoid paying taxes on this different type of payout plan. This particular plan also enables people to not owe Federal or State income taxes. The very important factor here is the benefit can be designed to pass to the surviving spouse unlike Social Security where the lower of the two spousal benefits stops at the death of the first spouse and the death benefit is a whopping $255.00. There is no way to use this $255.00 to replace the $18,000 - $30,000 per year of the passing spouses annual benefit payout.

If you look back at where the cost of living adjustments were over the last 30 years, the average is 4%. Over the last 20, the average is 2.4%. In 10 years, it's averaged about 2-1/2% and the last 5 which really puts the writing on the wall, the average is right at about 1.36%. There's obviously a pattern forming. The reality is the government is realizing the promised benefit program is in trouble and the political pressure on making sure to take care of our retirees. So one way they do that is by reducing the amount of our payout benefits over time with lower inflation adjustments.

So we have 'T' for *taxes*, 'I' for *inflation* and now the big 'M' in T.I.M.E. is for *market losses*. The fact that the Federal Reserve has obviously stimulated interest rates to such a low level in this country by a design that's forced the returns on once viewed safe savings vehicles like CD's, money market accounts, etc. that have been averaging under 1% which has forced many who swore off the stock market (that now has proof it is rigged as assumed by many for years) no more risking losing money again to the stock market. These low rates have also made many feel very nervous knowing they are spending down their principal by staying in these low yielding positions.

Looking at the fact that a lot of people's 401(k)s have turned into 201(k)s because of what's happened with the great recession, we've now have a lot of people very concerned about the stock market which is continuing to be very volatile. This brings us to the 'E' in T.I.M.E. which stands for *economic uncertainty.*

We now have a global economy, which means, if somebody breathes wrong overseas or if an emerging market looks to be volatile, all of a sudden it has a direct correlation to more uncertainty in our stock and bond markets here domestically in the United States. This is why you're seeing the market especially over these last five years, have major swings, up and down.

As a result of all this, it's forced people to say, "you know, maybe I really should look at this Social Security thing," because either they're in a crisis and it's a necessity, or some are learning that it can also be a very unique retirement tool if they understand that there are different strategies that would benefit them.

Susan: Let me see if I can recap what I heard you say. It's not such a simple equation of should I take my Social Security at 62 or not, is it? There's a lot of moving parts here because you're saying, taxes are not going down and actually more likely they're going to be pushed even higher. Between higher taxes and the cost of living adjustments getting smaller every year, then add in all the economic uncertainty in the world today, it makes for a very stressful time.

Chuck: Yea, that's right. The fact is this is no time to procrastinate retirement planning. Now is the T.I.M.E. to get serious about long term planning as 62 sneaks up on us and many are finding themselves without any real plan. It is important to understand the top threats also to Social Security itself, which are:

- Reduction in cost of living increases.

- Taxable amount of our income calculated toward taxes into the program. It used to be just the first 87,000 was counted as the max we were taxed for Social Security and today we are up to 117,000. A much faster increase than the cost of living 1.5% given for 2013!

- Percentage of tax on wages. Ex. Started as a promise of no tax to then 2% and now 6.2% Self-employed 12.4%!

- Full retirement age for higher social security benefits being pushed out to age 68-70 like the rumor Medicare full benefits age to be pushed out from 65 to 68!

Bottom line is this; many will and do need 50-60% of their retirement income to come from beyond Social Security benefits. About half of all retirees retirement income needed to live is placing their lifestyle at risk without a proven plan with a track record of measurable results which exist but is what is lacking for the majority of retirees!

Here Are Some of the Mistakes People Make When They Approach 62...

Susan: Can you share with us Chuck, what are some of the mistakes you see people make when they approach the age of 62?

Chuck: People are living longer and longer because of all the medical advancements in health-care today. That's great news. However, if someone elects to take their Social Security at 62 or even 66, 67, it's very likely at least one spouse in a couple will live to be age 96 and statistically speaking, it's over 52% odds that it will be the wife. So electing to take benefits early and therefore receiving a lot less over their lifetime could be a big mistake for many couples. People are prolonging their lives from eating healthier to exercising more and obviously, diseases and other health issues are now more and more treatable.

When you think about cost of living, the reality is if we take true inflation and true inflation which would include food and energy, we're going to project that number to be 6%. If we look at world inflation, we look at not just goods inflation like a lot of people think about what eggs, and bread, and gas costs, we also look at service inflation which is ultimately what retirees experience being kind of a game changer. Once they do retire, ultimately they're going to consume more services than just goods. Service inflation has averaged about 7.5% for the last 15 years. The moral of the story is that we teach what's called the rule of 72's. It's just a simple and basic economic formula. It says whatever number you divide into 72 tells you how quickly that number will double. If we take 6% into 72, that number is going to double in 12 years.

Twelve years, that means if you take a couple or an individual who's living on let's say for simplicity, $6,000 a month today, then it will eventually take 12 years from today for $12,000 to have the same purchasing power as what $6,000 had. A lot of people don't really have their arms around that. To challenge them in a way to get them to see that picture, I'll say, "Well, think about your first home and your first car and now think about your last home and your last car." If I'm working with somebody, let's say, in their early to mid-60s like a lot of our clients, they'll say, "Well, my goodness that's like a ten times multiple."

I say, "Yeah, you're getting the point." The reality is their first car may have been $3,500 and their last car was $35,000 or their first home was $35,000 and their last home was $350,000. That tells you how impactful the cost of living is and the challenge becomes if Social Security just gives a whopping 1.5% increase, we see this downward trend of where it used to average 4% and now it's averaging less than 1.5%. That's not going to maintain somebody's purchasing power and keep in mind the average retiree has 42% of their retirement income coming from Social Security alone!

The government is going to have a tough road to hoe because the only way you're going to really be able to maintain that program is to increase taxation.

The rates of taxation are based on tax brackets, the percentage of those that are paying in the Social Security taxation as it relates to a higher percentage of their income and then ultimately what percentage of Social Security benefits are going to be taxed. Since the time of the starting of the program back in the '30s when social security was created, the promise was it would never be taxed. Then it was taxed up to 50% and then it was promised to never go higher than the current 85%. When the cost of living increase force us to withdraw more to maintain our preferred standard of living this forces people to withdraw a higher amount from their IRA's or former employer 401(k)s and this higher withdraw will easily push the client above the threshold that will enable the IRS to tax up to 85% of their social security. This also puts the client at risk of running out of money before running out of life with the cost of living going up over one's lifetime as statistics today project the surviving spouse will live into her late 90's.

If someone's cost of living is going to double roughly every 12 years, then they're going to be forced to take more money out of their IRAs and 401(k)s because that's how they were taught to save. So not factoring the tax into the equation is a big mistake.

Here Are the Five Greatest Traps to Retirement...

By taking a higher withdrawal because of the higher taxation that's going to be required to come off the top just so they can net the amount that's going to be able to help them maintain their preferred standard of living, it's going to keep forcing them to pay the highest percentage of taxation on their Social Security which is ultimately going to be a double whammy. Here are the 5 greatest T.R.A.P.S. to retirement. *Taxes* are the 'T' in TRAPS. Taxes are going to be rising. I mean they are definitely going up to cover the short fall to programs like social security and Medicare.

The 'R' in TRAPS is *risk* of losses. If people realize that they're going to have to start taking down or distributing a much higher percentage based on the fact that their taxes have now gone up, they've got less from their Social Security benefits.

If people start having to draw more from the stock market, it's going to give the appearance to other people that there must be something wrong with the stock market. Just like anything, if people typically follow the crowd, if they start to see a selloff, now, all of a sudden, it's going to give the appearance as if the market's more volatile and then add in the fact that our economy is more volatile as it becomes a global economy, the risk of losses is going to be a big mess going forward because we're losing so much money in the market.

A big danger people have not planned for is called forced RMD's. (Required Minimum Distributions). This is a government allowed regulation that forces people that have saved in tax deferral programs like 401k's, 403b's, IRA's, SEP's, etc... to be forced to take a certain percentage as distributions by the end of each year or face a 50% penalty for not doing so. The penalty is based on the required distribution amount. Assume your required distribution amount is $20,000; the penalty is $10,000 or 50% of the forced required distribution! RMD should stand for "Retirement Money Drain!"

You still owed the tax on the $20,000 regardless of whether you took it or not. You're still going to have to pay the 50% penalty so that 'R' in TRAPS, _risk_ of losses is also risk of losses to the taxation because all retirees over 70.5 are forced to withdraw a required percentage of savings from their IRA's. Add to the fact the market losses to the average retiree or pre-retiree's retirement savings has been annihilated multiple times over the last 20 years. This is why a third of retirees today are reliant upon Social Security income for 42% of all their income from their Social Security benefit. No one really factored into their planning the fact that gas and groceries paid for 10-20 years ago are costing a lot more to them today and will cost a lot more tomorrow. That brings us to the 'A' in T.R.A.P.S., _annual inflation_ impact, the fact that it costs so much more to maintain the same lifestyle. I interviewed a gentleman working at Wal-Mart, a really interesting guy that retired from corporate America back in the 90's.

I asked him, "How many years ago did you retire?" He said, "I've been retired since 1996." I said if you don't mind me asking "Why do you work here?" He said, "Well, to be real honest with you it just costs more to maintain what my wife and I have. I did what a lot of us did, I went out and I bought a second home."

He's got another home up in the Knoxville, Tennessee area, on a lake. He said, "It costs so much more to be able to maintain the house now. The property taxes have gone up. The insurance has gone up. The utilities have gone up. He then said, "I needed to find more income as my pension hasn't kept up with the cost of living. I had to pick up another job in retirement that I didn't foresee doing. They're only paying me $7.50 an hour but the number of hours I'm able to get is what's enabling me to afford and keep the lake house."

I said, "Well, have you ever thought about not keeping it?" He said, "Well, you know it's one of the things where we want to keep it in the family. It's got pretty good equity over all these years even though property values have lost a lot. We want to be able to pass it on to our kids." I think what's happening is there's a real annual inflation impact and many people that are already experiencing it and for those people ultimately that haven't really thought it through. The cost to live will only become greater over time.

Then we come to the 'P', _personal health_ _setbacks_. The 'P' in our T.R.A.P.S. is that nobody ever plans on getting sick and yet unfortunately, it may not even be themselves that gets sick.

It could be a spouse or it could be their parents or ultimately, it could even be their children. We have one client who's got a great aunt, his wife's last family member. They want to be able to take care of her and here's a woman who's 102 years old and rides a bike 10 minutes a day, yet now she needs round the clock care. She has said "I would have never believed if someone told me in my 60's to prepare myself to live 40 plus years or four decades in retirement!" We all want to be in a position to help our loved ones, but our retirement funds are threatened due to these retirement T.R.A.P.S.

The 'S' stands for *serious longevity*. Not only are people getting sick but the cost to be able to maintain that is going up with Obamacare, Medicare and of course certain things that aren't covered through prescription drugs with Part D in Medicare. 'S' is for serious longevity due to a percentage of the population, centenarians who are the fastest growing segment of the population. People used to laugh when you talked about somebody living to age 100.

Another threat is the lesser of the two Social Security's goes away when the first spouse passes. We have a recent widow who shared, "Wow, what an impact." Her husband passed away due to stage four lung cancer this past fall. We sat down with her and said, "Look, let's redo your budget. We want to know your lifestyle income number. Don't lie about your L.I. we joke and say. Figure out your lifestyle income number and be real about it." I think a lot of people don't realize how much more they're spending because it's not ultimately something that a retiree typically sits around and looks at every day.

Another thing that gets overlooked as I have mentioned is there's only a death benefit from Social Security of $255. That clearly hasn't been inflation adjusted since the mid-'30s when it was created.

She said, "Chuck, between the loss of her late husband's pension because it wasn't a 100% survivor pension benefit and the loss of her Social Security since his Social Security was greater. She's had a $2,000 a month swing which panicked her. She's like, "Look, I know you talk about this. I know you wrote about this." She's been a client of mine for three years. She said, "Reality has really set in for me. I really want to re-analyze because I didn't realize what a hole that $2,000 a month has really put into my lifestyle."

I think one of the biggest dangers or traps as I just shared is that no one is really analyzing retirement income solutions when you think about people who help people financially, ultimately it's all about, "Where's your money and how much better can we make it grow or how much more can we do to prevent any more major losses that you can't withstand?" But there's so much more to it than that.

A retirement strategist helps people discover and uncover the different areas of their hidden wealth. Social Security as 42% of a retiree's income is coming from this particular source.

It's not really a secret. It's hidden. It's hidden because no one's really ever educated people on what are the best Social Security filing strategies to use. Again, one strategy may be right for you and may be completely different for somebody else. The important point is to understand your own customized filing strategy that shows where and how one can maximize their benefit. Sometimes that may mean ultimately creating a very unique, more personalized strategy and just leveraging the Social Security benefit to create a bigger benefit for them. Some of it may be as simple as just strategizing on certain terminology that we teach such as file and suspend, or file and restrict.

After some of our clients learn these strategies, they're educating the Social Security Administration when they call them. The Social Security Administration's not educating our client. Again, they're an order-taker not a wealth-maker or a wealth-protector if you will. As a result, I think the biggest concern out there is that people don't realize what an important retirement income source Social Security is.

Social security is part of the industry discussion on retirement being a three-legged stool. One leg is Social Security. We now know Social Security supports the average retiree's income by almost half (42% average). The other two legs come from pensions (many don't have or will not have a pension to fall back on) and retirement savings. Most have not saved enough especially reflected in a recent study at Boston College's department of retirement research reflecting the average retirement savings income generated is only $575.00 monthly!

A lot of people are realizing they've put their entire financial future into the hands of a program that ultimately isn't looking out for the consumer first but will likely represent half their retirement income.

As much as it may be a tough pill to swallow for people that will read this, it's a retirement reality. There is a reason why you're locked out of your 401(k) and IRA until your 59-1/2. There's a reason why you're forced out of that money at 70-1/2 and why we don't get the full retirement age benefits till 66 or 67. This is the clever way to become taxed on a higher portion of our income and social security.

Right now, another big danger in retirement is Medicare. Medicare is not like Social Security where it's not a progressive age or tax program. In other words, automatically today when somebody turns 65 they get full Medicare benefits.

There's been a lot of talk and rumor that we'll also have a full benefit required age for full Medicare benefits. That rumor now is age 69 so maybe somebody elects to take Medicare at 65 but they're only going to get let's say 75% of the benefit unless they prolong that till age 69. You've got a lot of people out there that are very concerned about this added expense not factored into their retirement income needs. They are worried over this and other added expenses like prescription medications that are more expensive plus the additional amount they will need to pay out of pocket since what will likely get covered is going to be less.

You just got a lot of people that if they'll take the time to your original question what is the best strategy? A strategy is getting with somebody who ultimately understands what I call the retirement second half of the game. Learning to properly position one into retirement is key!

I think a lot of people are having a tough time distinguishing between a retirement specialist who understands Medicare and Social Security and long term care and Personal Protected Pension Planning as opposed to 99% of who hold their shingle out there that say, "Hey, put your money with us. We can really help your money grow and hopefully not lose any more of it than you have to."

It's just a different real world retirement dynamic I don't think a lot of people realize until they get to that point of really getting serious about having a proven retirement strategy with a track record of measurable results. For many it starts with the harsh reality they have to change their thinking. A great example is learning how to have their retirement savings out fox inflation without exposing their retirement savings to serious losses. The harsh reality of this is what the average person lost in '08 in the market, Susan; it's going to take on average 13-1/2 years to get back to even. A lot of people, they're looking at this and they've made a couple of dire strait choices. They've said, "I'll never go back into the market and they put their money into cash. Then they see what the federal government's done to artificially stimulate interest rates which then forces them back into the market because interest rates are so low they are forced back into the market to have a chance of making any real interest.

They're spending down their principal at a record pace and yet they don't really know if it's safe to get back into the market because, of course, it looks as if 2013 was just this magical year. Already we see going into 2014, the market's still very volatile. It had about a 700 point swing just in one week so now they're saying, "Oh, gosh. That doesn't look to be the same trend so I probably shouldn't dip my foot back in the water too soon."

You've got other people who are saying, "Well, this stock market is going to keep running. I can't afford to leave my money in the bank or low interest yielding and volatile bond programs." They're going to be deeply disappointed when they realize that most of all of these once safe savings vehicles to save their retirement money in will continue to pay very little interest, or no interest like today based on the Federal Reserve trying to keep our economy afloat, due to the fact that the government's in trouble and needs the economy to get back to growing. In fact, here are the facts: Fewer people are employed causing taxation to be way down, the largest number of people are retiring in our history, and unemployment is way up.

And unfortunately, you've got a lot of the media, I think, misleading people to believe that things in our economy are rosier than what they really are. Because the reality is things are not rosy. People ultimately need to plan differently because we live in a very different economy that requires a new path for protected retirement planning.

Why It's not Too Late for You…

Susan: So you're suggesting you shouldn't use the same strategies that got you *to* retirement *in* retirement? Is that correct?

Chuck: Yes, Retirement planning is a different half of the game and requires different planning design. People preparing to retire or those already retired are finding they can't take the risks of losing any more money. Statistics prove many pre-retirees and retirees have not saved enough or many have lost enough that they can't afford any significant loss and be able to sustain the income required to support their preferred lifestyle. Market data research also find a large percentage of pre-retirees and retirees are not aware of how much will be needed in retirement savings to support and sustain them and the surviving spouse throughout their lifetime. This current retirement generation is the first generation that will spend more years not working than the number of years they worked and will need their retirement savings to last 30-40 years!

There are a core four retirement success criteria that are required in order to not just survive but to be able to thrive in retirement we created an acronym to describe as S.A.F.E. How do you get your retirement money safe? S.A.F.E., the 'S' stands for *secure from* _losses_. People need to understand there are programs and strategies that allow your money to participate only when the market goes up not when it goes down. You get so many people that are very distrusting of Wall Street or insurance companies or to any products they might automatically say, "Well, that sounds too good to be true. I don't want to risk another Ponzi scheme."

These are programs of the supported pensions whether we're talking about teacher pensions or professional sport pensions or major corporation pensions for hundreds of years for that matter but they are S.A.F.E, secure from losses. The 'A' in S.A.F.E stands for _accessibility_, access when you need it. This way someone's not locked out of their money till they're 59-1/2 or they're not forced out of their money when they turn 70-1/2.

They can get to it when they need it but the money is able to earn a very respectable higher than inflation interest rate. In fact, some of these programs have averaged 8.50 to 10.25% over the last 20 years which is likely the worst two decades since the great depression. Yet people have never been made aware of these proven programs but ironically these programs are the biggest pension protection programs in every major bank and corporation across the United States. Yet they've never been made aware of them.

The 'F' which I think is the big one is _freedom from taxation_. See, if we realize that taxes are going to have to go up, then it's really going to threaten people to the point to where they now have to start taking out more from their *IRA's* to net the same. Barring some major economic meltdown like we obviously have had (and another predicted soon by the great Warren Buffet) in 2008-2009 or 2000-2001 and 2002. Many if not most will be out of money in 7 to 11 years. I mean their money is gone and it will not be coming back again.

Then the 'E', I think both husband and wife appreciate this one in particular, *ease of management*. When I sit with couples that are retired or maybe one of the two spouses are retired, they say to me, "I just don't want to do this anymore. I don't want to have to see the market futures open or how the overseas market's close and what impact that's having on my brokerage account minute by minute"

I've got people, Susan, I've met with that have said, "You know, I figured what the heck, I might as well take the wheel because I can lose this money just as well as the person I was paying to lose it and have more fun doing it". Even though that's funny and not so funny, this is what a lot of these folks are saying, I just don't want to do it anymore." What we hear their spouse saying is "I'm so sick and tired of pulling up this account trying to figure how we are doing? What's it look like today? Are we up today? Are we down today? Are we going to be able to take the kids and the grand-kids to Disneyland or did the market get walloped?"

That's really no way to be retired. The reality is retirement based on Webster's definition is defined as 'put out of use'. Nobody wants to be put out of use. We want to have purpose and we want to be able to do the things we enjoy and we find a lot of our clients really want to travel and they want to be there at their grand-children's sporting events and school events, and plays, and all that fun stuff. They want to be more involved in the hobbies they like and so ease of management is important where they don't have to monitor daily or weekly the ups and downs of their life savings. It's just simple for them to know their retirement savings only participates when the market index goes up and never have to worry about their savings when the market index goes down.

In summary they want their money to be secure from loses, accessible when they need it, free from taxation and has ease of management. If more people understood this, they could use their Social Security benefits to fund their <u>own</u> Social Security, their own Personal Protected Pension Plan. This would be just another area that instead of counting on the hopeful future promises of the federal government to count on proven hundred plus year old promises with built in protection programs and avoid the government changing the rules like the government does with programs like Social Security cost of living adjustment based off of the manipulative factors of what the government defined as inflation and use the numbers that they choose to use to determine if our benefits will be increased or not.

This is a chance for people to say, let me take the management of this, take this money and put it into programs that have proven to do what they say they're going to do without the contract being able to be changed like the government does all the time with our social security calculations.

What Is One Filing Strategy Most Couples Do not Know that Could Cost Them Over $200K?

I think it starts with getting folks educated on where can you get the highest benefit payout based on what the husband or the wife elects to do and at what age? Because there are some benefits of drawing early and there are some benefits of deferring and drawing later. There are over eighty different filing combinations to choose from. One client recently shared with us, "Wow! I had no idea that there were these unique filing strategies." One example that we teach is what we call the $212,000 mistake. The average husband and wife leave an excess of $212,000 on the table by not knowing a simple file, suspend and file and then restrict switching formula.

Susan: Can you share what the strategy is?

Chuck: Yeah, File, Restrict and Switch! Let's use a recent example where the husband is 70 and the wife is 66. The wife in this scenario will want to file a restricted application after the husband files and suspends, that way she can use the 50% spousal benefit because if she doesn't restrict her application she can't use the switching strategy to get her higher payout with the annual 8% increase and cost of living added to it when she switches from the spousal benefit for the last four years and collects her age 70 benefit adjusted higher payout amount!

People don't realize every year somebody delays taking their Social Security, at least as of today, the Social Security benefit goes up 8% a year. People would be very hard pressed to get a guaranteed 8% in the stock market, if they understood this file and suspend strategy. Another great strategy is if a person is divorced and as long as they were married for 10 years or longer, they can use a very unique filing strategy with file and suspend and ultimately increase their pay out. Most don't even know about this. No one is going to tell them because they or their advisers don't know. The adviser doesn't get compensation in their mind for sharing in Social Security benefit filing strategies. Let me ask you, if one claims to have a financial adviser and a retirement plan, how could they if what will likely represent 25%-50% of their total retirement income source never have been discussed let alone strategized?

Well we'll show someone where they can increase their benefit $500 to $1500 that translates into an additional $200,000 or more in lifetime benefits. I mean that especially in the economy we live in today, $500 to $1500 a month, there's a big, big swing. This is an example people aren't aware of what they're not aware of. People are not aware that they're leaving $6,000 to $18,000 a year on the table a year. One spouse today is projected to live to age 96, while it is also projected the average surviving spouse will live ten to fifteen years past the passing of the first spouse and these payout amount will make a significant difference. One can understand the significant difference in the additional $6,000 to $18,000 a year for 30 years and run the math and you see what somebody leaves on the table.

In fact, we have an interesting case. The case study in our webinar that teaches about a couple that was going to leave an excess of $386,000 on the table by not learning their filing strategy.

Susan: Right. There's no one like you said, in the Social Security office, who is sharing this information. People don't know what they don't know, so they need this guidance. What if you're single, Chuck? Is there any special strategies if you're single going into retirement?

Chuck: We call it the Yo-yo plan which stands for "you're on your own". We find a lot of folks who are single; we think it's even more imperative they have a strategy as there won't be a survivor pension benefit for them.

Obviously, we talked about if there's only one Social Security benefit, it's not like there's two to draw from when somebody's single. We think it's as much if not more important for somebody who's single to start realizing and ultimately using their Social Security to build their own Personal Protected Pension Plan especially if they have children, who receive a whopping $255 death benefit from their

Social Security.

Once they pass, a lot of single folks may have an interest in leaving money to their children, their church or even a charity. There are ways where they could use the Social Security benefit to fund something while they're still working, to go ahead and elect those benefits so that they build in their own Personal Protective Pension Plan with inflation protection. Being able to leave 3 to 5 times what they were able to put back into those plans and draw anywhere from two to four times the amount of income that ultimately Social Security would've paid them.

We think it's very important for those that are not married or never have been married to really be looking at alternative approaches to retirement with utilization of their Social Security benefits.

Single clients can learn how they can leverage their social security benefit into something that's going to pay a greater payout of income. In addition, being able to leave a lot more money to the people they care about once they pass.

We have what we have significantly trained in the specialty are of lifetime retirement income planning what is known as a authorized Hidden Wealth Architect. This special training retirement specialist fully understands the most advanced strategies for maximum income for wealth creation and preservation.

It's just very important that all pre-retirees

especially if one wants to focus on trying to really ramp up their income before they retire. A lot of people don't realize the taxation of 50% to 85% of their Social Security and the real impact of this tax reducing their spendable retirement income.

There's ways that you can eliminate having any of your Social Security taxed by using some of these proven alternative approaches to retirement income planning.

Here's Exactly How the Social Security Pay Out Maximization Plan Works...

Susan: Right, very good. If someone wants to know more information or wants to know how this all works, what do they need to do?

Chuck: Get educated. One of the things that we find is how one can turn decades into a day of learning? There is a great educational webinar for people to attend. People can simply go to www.WhatToDoAt62.com; there is an industry leading expert on the subject of maximizing Social Security benefits. It really helps people understand all these fancy filing strategies and complicated jargon around the subject of Social Security. In under an hour, they can glean the basics and really learn their choices and best option as they become more knowledgeable and apply their new knowledge so it becomes wisdom.

Starting with the one hour webinar is best. Get

educated and learn the best strategy as it relates to their own individual situation.

www.WhatToDoAt62.com will enable them to know far more about Social Security just by watching and participating in this educational webinar.

One of the first things in the webinar teaches people how to find what benefits you would be looking at receiving. Right after the webinar people can elect to request a customized benefit maximization payout report. What we found from the feedback is it really opens up people's eyes to say, "Wow! I didn't realize I could be leaving, on average, an excess of $200,000 on the table."

Maybe they're not going to start drawing those benefits right away or the spouse will start drawing those benefits for a couple of years. People miss that fact that the average couple is going to draw somewhere between $1-2 million over their lifetime from Social Security. When you realize the average boomer has saved only $50,000 towards retirement, their social security is the highest benefit pay out but ultimately they may understand the least about it.

What you don't know about Social Security is ultimately far more important than what you feel you do know. Which is why I think by just starting with the webinar and learning what they don't know about Social Security would be a great starting point.

If they want more education, they can learn how simple it is to get their benefits and then how simple it is to plug their numbers into a unique software platform to show people if you did this, you could get this. If you did this, you could get this much more. It's very eye opening for people to see the different amounts.

It provides a diagram detail on what was answered which shows this is when you should really file. It's one of those three potential age choices that they have but then it documents proof why and how to get the highest income payout benefits. People can take that information and apply it however they choose but at least they're going to be educated with the facts.

Here's Exactly How to Get Your Social Security Pay Out Maximization Plan...

Susan: Right. You're saying you have a process where they answer some questions about their situation, and then your software shows their personalized highest income payout?

Chuck: We call it The Social Security Pay Out Maximization Plan. The process is very simple.

Susan: They answer some questions and your special software program calculates for them what their options are so they can make the best choice. That's quite brilliant actually.

Chuck: In summary those interested in learning more can simply go to www.WhatToDat62.com to register for the educational webinar unless they are ready to get their customized plan design. The time is now as I was just sent a article from Market Watch titled _"Time To Close The Social Security Loophole"._ The article discusses the governments focus on eliminating aggressive claiming strategies.

The unique filing strategies today may not be available in the future as the program is being tweaked daily it seems. We have many eager to get their best filing strategy determined before the opportunity is lost. Because of all the uncertainty and because of people finding themselves needing to make decisions about drawing Social Security long before they thought they were going to have to, we've had to add a third webinar time just to accommodate folks due to the demand. I think a lot of people don't realize even when you're conducting an educational webinar there is limited space. We've now added a third time slot so people don't get locked out.

There's just a simple survey at the end of the webinar asking if they would like to take the next step and looking at what their benefit choices would be, where to get those choices and then how to gain insight into a customized maximization plan as it relates to their own personal data. Then if they want to act on that information, they can act on that further and look at alternative approaches to utilizing the benefit even though they might not need it but could learn how to use their benefits for a better plan to create more income than what their Social Security income would be.

Susan: I love it. Wow! Thank you so much. This has been very eye-opening for me. I had no idea it was this involved. You hear about the three different years and you think it's a pretty straight forward simple choice but there's a lot more at stake.

Chuck: Yeah. The question to ask is, *Is what I don't know about Social Security more important than what I think I do know*?

If people remember just one thing, remember this question: *"Do I want to retire on my terms or the governments terms with changes the government can make out of my control?"*

What people don't know is far more important than what they think they do know. If they'll get educated, their eyes will be open.

Susan: Thank you Chuck for sharing this with us. I think anyone reading this will have their eyes open and want to know more. I know I did. Where can they go to get more information?

Chuck: Yes, they can go to www.WhatToDoAt62.com and then just follow the steps. They can just go at their own pace to get educated. It's strictly educational based so it's very simple and easy for them to access to get educated.

Susan: Very good. Well, thank you so much for sharing these strategies with us Chuck.

Chuck: I appreciate the opportunity to help people learn *What to Do at 62*.

Author Bio

Best-selling author Chuck Oliver is a nationally recognized Wealth Strategist who works with boomers & seniors who are uncertain about planning in and for retirement.

Their concerns center on taxes, market risk and the possibility of out-living their income.

Chuck helps clients gain direction, confidence and capability with the proven success of his model, The Hidden Wealth System.

He educates clients on how to increase their retirement income by 50% or more with little or no tax, with no market risk and how to establish a tax-free income for life that will transfer tax-free to future generation.

Chuck's accomplishments include:

- Best-selling author of <u>Power Principles for Success, Power a Tax-Free Financial Future</u> and <u>Game Changers; America's Leading Entrepreneurs</u>

- Fox TV News financial contributor

- National Radio Show Host of Hidden Wealth Radio

Here's How To Get Your Maximum Social Security Benefit Income Plan Designed and Maximize Your Payout...

You want to make sure you don't make any missteps when electing your benefits. The confusing part is not knowing how to maximize your Social Security Income payout so you don't leave money on the table month after month and year after year.

That's where we come in. We help people just like you structure a customized Social Security Maximization Income plan which translates into $100,000 to $500,000 in additional benefit payouts to you and your spouse.

Step 1: We invest 20 minutes understanding where you are, what your benefits are and when makes the most sense to start your Social Security Benefits. We simplify your understanding of What to Do at 62.

Step 2: We help you discover and uncover the key strategies used to maximize your Social Security Income and how to avoid paying up to 85% tax on your Social Security Benefits.

Step 3: We take it from there and design your Personal Social Security Maximization Plan.

Most people are not aware of these key Social Security filing strategies. We turn people's lack of awareness of Social Security Benefits into an easy to understand education which empowers you to have the greatest payout plan.

Let's get to work, just send an email to:

Help@WhatToDoAt62.com and we will take it from there.

www.ingramcontent.com/pod-product-compliance
Lightning Source LLC
Chambersburg PA
CBHW071826170526
45167CB00003B/1444